Fractions: Concepts and Problem Solving
Grade 4

Table of Contents

Fractions: Concepts and Problem Solving
Grade 4

Introduction

Helping students form an understanding of fractions is a challenging process. To best accomplish the task, educators must approach the subject in a way that is meaningful to students. Moreover, the National Council of Teachers of Mathematics (NCTM) has indicated that "students should build their understanding of fractions as parts of a whole and as division." (*Principles and Standards for School Mathematics*, page 150.) *Fractions: Concepts and Problem Solving* serves as a companion to the classroom mathematics curriculum and encompasses many of the standards established by the NCTM for this grade level. (Refer to the correlation chart below.) The book is divided into four units: Concept Development, Computation, Problem Solving, and Enrichment. Each page targets a specific skill to help bolster students who need additional work in a particular area.

Unit 1: Concept Development
The pages in this unit use a variety of learning styles to help students understand the fundamental principles of fractions. Students identify fractions that are parts of wholes, parts of groups, and mixed numbers. They also compare and order fractions.

Unit 2: Computation
Here, students are introduced to the steps necessary to calculate fractional algorithms using visuals. Practice exercises on most pages use models to guide students. Toward the end of the page, students work the problems without models. Students work to find the simplest form, to add and subtract fractions with like denominators, and to add and subtract fractions with unlike denominators.

Unit 3: Problem Solving
Students work word problems and real-life application problems to further develop skills using fractions. They work with patterns, bar graphs, line graphs, and circle graphs to find fractional relationships. They also explore basic probability.

Unit 4: Enrichment
To challenge and extend learning, students explore basic algebra principles, decimals, money, and geometry.

Special Note
We encourage the use of manipulatives for acquisition of skills with fractions. Examples include, but are not limited to, the following: Fraction Bars®, Fraction Tiles®, Fraction Builder® Strips, Rainbow Fraction Circles and Squares®, Fraction Stax®, and Fraction Burger®.

Notes

Assessment
There are two kinds of assessment pages.
- On pages 5 and 6 is a general assessment that covers important fraction skills appropriate for fourth grade. It can be given as a pretest to gauge students' knowledge of fractions. Later in the year, the same test can be administered to determine students' understanding, progress, and achievement.
- The first three units also have an assessment. They can be administered at any time during the unit as a pretest, review, or posttest for specific fraction concepts.

NCTM Standards Correlation
The NCTM Standards Correlation chart below identifies a variety of mathematics standards that are appropriate for the study of fractions.

Fraction Table
A Fraction Table can be found on page 3. Students can use the graphic organizer to quickly identify and compare fractions. You may wish to photocopy two pages for each student. One copy can be cut apart and used for fractions strips.

Fraction Circles
Fraction circles representing basic fractions are on page 4. Make a copy for each student. Students can cut them apart and use the circles as manipulatives while they work. You may wish to provide envelopes for students to store cut pieces.

NCTM Standards Correlation

Numbers and Operations: 8, 9, 10, 11, 13, 14, 15, 16, 17, 18, 19, 20, 21, 22, 23, 24, 25, 26, 27, 28, 29, 30, 31, 32, 33, 34, 35, 36, 38, 39, 40, 41, 42, 44, 45

Algebra: 11, 13, 20, 33, 42

Geometry: 8, 9, 12, 43, 46

Measurement: 11, 20, 31, 32, 34, 35, 36, 37, 45

Data Analysis and Probability: 30, 31, 34, 38, 39, 40, 41

Problem Solving: 30, 31, 32, 37, 38, 39, 40, 41, 42, 43, 44, 45, 46

Fraction Table

1											
$\frac{1}{2}$		$\frac{1}{3}$	$\frac{1}{4}$	$\frac{1}{5}$	$\frac{1}{6}$	$\frac{1}{7}$	$\frac{1}{8}$	$\frac{1}{9}$	$\frac{1}{10}$	$\frac{1}{11}$	$\frac{1}{12}$

Fraction Circles

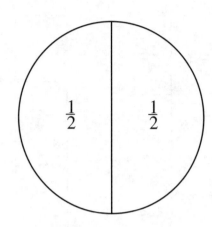

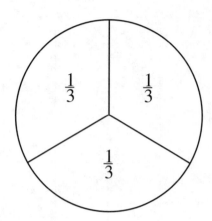

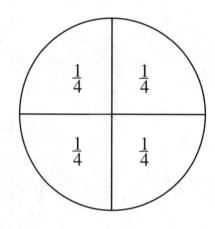

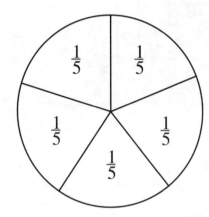

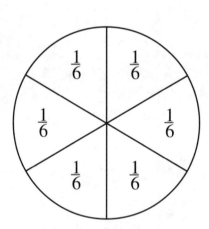

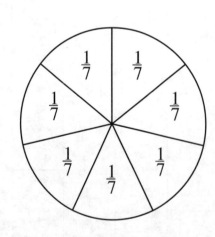

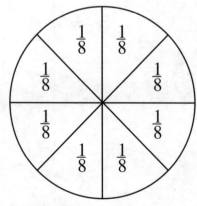

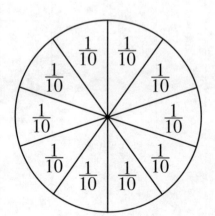

Name _____   Date _____

General Assessment

Darken the circle by the correct answer.

1. Which shaded area shows $\frac{2}{3}$?

   Ⓐ A
   Ⓑ B
   Ⓒ C
   Ⓓ D

   A   **B**   **C**   **D**

2. What fraction shows the part of this figure that is shaded?

   Ⓐ $\frac{2}{8}$
   Ⓑ $\frac{28}{10}$
   Ⓒ $\frac{28}{100}$
   Ⓓ $2\frac{8}{10}$

   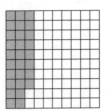

3. Which shaded part shows the greatest fraction?

   Ⓐ ▦ $= \frac{4}{6}$ Ⓑ ▭ $= \frac{1}{3}$

   Ⓒ ▦ $= \frac{8}{9}$ Ⓓ ▭ $= \frac{1}{2}$

4. What fraction shows how much of this group is shaded?

   Ⓐ $1\frac{9}{10}$
   Ⓑ $1\frac{1}{10}$
   Ⓒ $\frac{11}{9}$
   Ⓓ $\frac{11}{11}$

   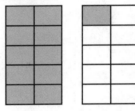

5. Change $\frac{8}{3}$ into a mixed number.

   Ⓐ $8\frac{1}{3}$
   Ⓑ $5\frac{2}{3}$
   Ⓒ $2\frac{2}{3}$
   Ⓓ $1\frac{1}{3}$

6. Which fraction is <u>not</u> equivalent to $\frac{1}{4}$?

   Ⓐ $\frac{2}{8}$
   Ⓑ $\frac{5}{20}$
   Ⓒ $\frac{3}{12}$
   Ⓓ $\frac{5}{16}$

7. Which fraction names the simplest form of $\frac{6}{9}$?

   Ⓐ $\frac{1}{3}$
   Ⓑ $\frac{2}{3}$
   Ⓒ $\frac{2}{5}$
   Ⓓ $\frac{3}{3}$

8. How many inches are there between point B and point A?

   Ⓐ $1\frac{1}{2}$ inches
   Ⓑ 3 inches
   Ⓒ 1 inch
   Ⓓ $2\frac{1}{2}$ inches

Go on to the next page.

9. $\frac{3}{8}$
$+\frac{3}{8}$

Ⓐ $\frac{1}{8}$

Ⓑ $\frac{1}{2}$

Ⓒ $\frac{2}{3}$

Ⓓ $\frac{3}{4}$

10. $\frac{5}{9}$
$-\frac{1}{3}$

Ⓐ $\frac{4}{6}$

Ⓑ $\frac{2}{9}$

Ⓒ $\frac{3}{9}$

Ⓓ $\frac{3}{4}$

11. $7\frac{3}{7} + 2\frac{2}{7} = $ _____

Ⓐ $10\frac{2}{7}$

Ⓑ $9\frac{5}{7}$

Ⓒ $5\frac{2}{7}$

Ⓓ $5\frac{1}{7}$

12. $9\frac{4}{6} - 5\frac{1}{6} = $ _____

Ⓐ $4\frac{1}{2}$

Ⓑ $5\frac{1}{2}$

Ⓒ $4\frac{5}{6}$

Ⓓ $14\frac{5}{6}$

13. 6
$+\frac{3}{8}$

Ⓐ 7

Ⓑ $7\frac{3}{8}$

Ⓒ $6\frac{3}{8}$

Ⓓ 5

14. $4\frac{3}{4}$
$-\frac{1}{2}$

Ⓐ $4\frac{1}{2}$

Ⓑ $4\frac{1}{4}$

Ⓒ $3\frac{1}{2}$

Ⓓ $3\frac{1}{4}$

15. Kai's mother made 24 spring rolls for the school's food festival. One fourth of them were eaten by the first group of visitors. How many were eaten?

Ⓐ 18

Ⓑ 12

Ⓒ 6

Ⓓ 4

16. Laurel used $\frac{1}{2}$ cup of sugar in her apple muffins. Nina used $\frac{5}{8}$ cup of sugar in her apple muffins. How much more sugar did Nina use?

Ⓐ $\frac{3}{8}$

Ⓑ $\frac{1}{3}$

Ⓒ $\frac{1}{16}$

Ⓓ $\frac{1}{8}$

Assessment

Directions

Write a fraction for each model.

1.

_____

2.

_____

3.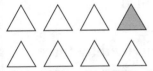

What part is shaded?

_____

4.

What part is on the log?

_____

Directions

Write three other ways that you can read or write each fraction.

5. $\frac{1}{2}$ _____

_____

_____

6. $\frac{3}{4}$ _____

_____

_____

Directions

Look at the first figure. Circle the figure that shows an equivalent fraction. Then, write the equivalent fractions.

7. 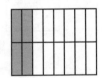 _____

Directions

Compare. Write <, >, or =.

8. $\frac{4}{10}$ ◯ $\frac{9}{10}$

9. $\frac{2}{4}$ ◯ $\frac{2}{6}$

Exploring Fractions

The fraction names a **part of a whole** apple.

$\frac{1}{2}$ of an apple is shaded.

Read: one half
one out of two
one divided by two

The fraction names a **part of a group** of apple trees.

$\frac{1}{3}$ of the apple trees have apples.

Read: one third
one out of three
one divided by three

Directions

Write *part of a whole* or *part of a group* for each example.

1.

$\frac{1}{4}$ _____

2.

$\frac{1}{5}$ _____

3.

$\frac{5}{7}$ _____

Directions

Circle the figures that show thirds.

4.

Directions

Write three other ways that you could read or write each fraction.

5. $\frac{1}{4}$ _____

_____

_____

6. $\frac{2}{3}$ _____

_____

_____

7. $\frac{4}{9}$ _____

_____

_____

Part of a Whole

A **fraction** is a number that names a part of a whole. The parts are all equal. The top number is the numerator. The bottom number is the denominator.

	$\dfrac{\text{shaded parts}}{\text{total parts}} = \dfrac{2}{4}$	**Read:** two fourths two out of four two divided by four
(circle divided into eighths, 3 shaded)	$\dfrac{\text{shaded parts}}{\text{total parts}} = \dfrac{3}{8}$	**Read:** three eighths three out of eight three divided by eight

Directions

Color the figures that show equal parts.

1.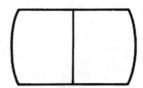

2.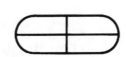

Directions

Write a fraction for each model.

3. $\dfrac{\text{shaded parts}}{\text{total parts}} = \dfrac{\Box}{\Box}$

4. $\dfrac{\text{shaded parts}}{\text{total parts}} = \dfrac{\Box}{\Box}$

5. $\dfrac{\text{shaded parts}}{\text{total parts}} = \dfrac{\Box}{\Box}$

6. 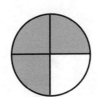 $\dfrac{\text{shaded parts}}{\text{total parts}} = \dfrac{\Box}{\Box}$

Part of a Group

A **fraction** can also name a part of a group.

	$\dfrac{\text{parts shaded}}{\text{number of equal parts}} = \dfrac{1}{2}$	**Read:** one half one out of two one divided by two
	$\dfrac{\text{parts shaded}}{\text{number of equal parts}} = \dfrac{2}{3}$	**Read:** two thirds two out of three two divided by three

Directions

Write a fraction for each model.

1.

   $\dfrac{\text{parts with cats}}{\text{number of equal parts}} = \dfrac{\square}{\square}$

2.

   $\dfrac{\text{parts with stars}}{\text{number of equal parts}} = \dfrac{\square}{\square}$

3. What part is swimming?

   _____

4. What part is flying?

   _____

Estimating Fractions

You can use a fraction bar to help you estimate fractions.

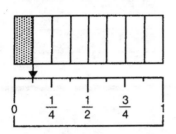

$\frac{1}{8}$ is about 0.

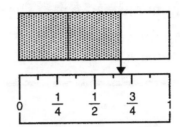

$\frac{2}{3}$ is about $\frac{1}{2}$.

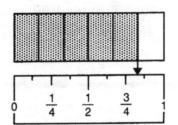

$\frac{5}{6}$ is about 1.

Directions

Use the fraction bar to estimate the shaded part of each. Write *about 0, about $\frac{1}{2}$, or about 1.*

1.

$\frac{4}{6}$ _____

2.

$\frac{1}{9}$ _____

3.

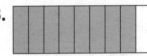

$\frac{8}{9}$ _____

Directions

Circle the better estimate.

4.

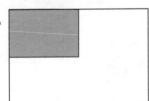

$\frac{1}{3}$ or $\frac{1}{4}$

5.

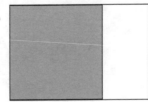

$\frac{1}{4}$ or $\frac{2}{3}$

6.

$\frac{1}{3}$ or $\frac{3}{4}$

Equal Parts

Two figures may be the same size and shape, but they may be divided into a different number of parts. The figures can be shaded to show equal amounts. Three out of 4 parts equals 6 out of 8 parts.

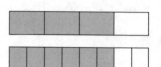

Directions

Write *equal* or *not equal* for each example.

1.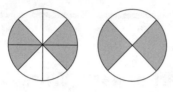

_____

2.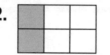

_____

3.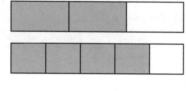

_____

4.

_____

5.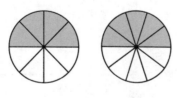

_____

6.

_____

Equivalent Fractions

$\frac{1}{3}$		$\frac{1}{3}$		$\frac{1}{3}$	
$\frac{1}{6}$	$\frac{1}{6}$	$\frac{1}{6}$	$\frac{1}{6}$	$\frac{1}{6}$	$\frac{1}{6}$
$\frac{1}{9}$ $\frac{1}{9}$ $\frac{1}{9}$		$\frac{1}{9}$ $\frac{1}{9}$ $\frac{1}{9}$		$\frac{1}{9}$ $\frac{1}{9}$ $\frac{1}{9}$	

Fractions that name the same amount are called **equivalent fractions.** $\frac{1}{3}$, $\frac{2}{6}$, and $\frac{3}{9}$ are different names for the same number. So, $\frac{1}{3} = \frac{2}{6} = \frac{3}{9}$, which makes them equivalent fractions.

Directions

Complete to find the equivalent fraction.

1.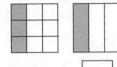

$$\frac{3}{9} = \frac{\square}{3}$$

2.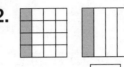

$$\frac{4}{16} = \frac{\square}{4}$$

3.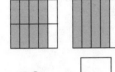

$$\frac{8}{10} = \frac{\square}{5}$$

4.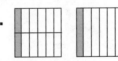

$$\frac{2}{12} = \frac{\square}{6}$$

Directions

Color the correct number of parts to show the equivalent fractions. Then, write the equivalent fraction.

5.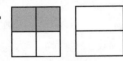

$$\frac{2}{4} = \frac{\square}{\square}$$

6.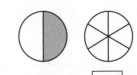

$$\frac{1}{2} = \frac{\square}{\square}$$

Comparing Fractions

You can compare fractions that have the same denominators.

Step 1: Compare $\frac{2}{5}$ and $\frac{3}{5}$.

Step 2: Compare the shaded areas in the fraction bars.

Step 3: 2 < 3, so $\frac{2}{5} < \frac{3}{5}$.

$\frac{2}{5}$

$\frac{3}{5}$

You can also compare fractions that have different denominators.

Step 1: Compare $\frac{2}{3}$ and $\frac{1}{2}$.

Step 2: Compare the shaded areas in the fraction bars.

Step 3: Since $\frac{2}{3}$ has a larger shaded area, $\frac{2}{3} > \frac{1}{2}$.

$\frac{2}{3}$

$\frac{1}{2}$

Directions

Compare. Write <, >, or =.

1.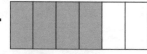

$\frac{4}{6} \bigcirc \frac{2}{6}$

2.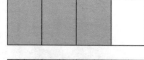

$\frac{3}{4} \bigcirc \frac{7}{8}$

3.

$\frac{2}{5} \bigcirc \frac{4}{10}$

Directions

Compare. Write <, >, or =.

4. $\frac{1}{4} \bigcirc \frac{2}{4}$

5. $\frac{1}{2} \bigcirc \frac{1}{4}$

6. $\frac{4}{10} \bigcirc \frac{9}{10}$

7. $\frac{4}{5} \bigcirc \frac{3}{5}$

8. $\frac{2}{6} \bigcirc \frac{2}{3}$

9. $\frac{2}{4} \bigcirc \frac{3}{6}$

Ordering Fractions

Sometimes you will need to order a set of fractions. To do this, compare two the fractions by using equivalent fractions. Write them in order using > or <. Then, compare them to the other fraction using equivalent fractions.

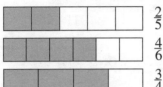

$$\frac{2}{5} < \frac{4}{6} < \frac{3}{4}$$

So, from least to greatest, the fraction order is $\frac{2}{5}, \frac{4}{6}, \frac{3}{4}$.

Directions

Write the fractions in order from least to greatest.

1.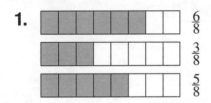

   _____

2.

   _____

3. $\frac{2}{5}, \frac{1}{5}, \frac{3}{5}$

   _____

4. $\frac{2}{6}, \frac{1}{4}, \frac{2}{5}$

   _____

5. $\frac{1}{6}, \frac{1}{3}, \frac{1}{2}$

   _____

6. $\frac{3}{4}, \frac{2}{3}, \frac{5}{8}$

   _____

7. What can you tell about fractions from Exercise 3?

   _____

   _____

8. What can you tell about fractions from Exercise 5?

   _____

   _____

Mixed Numbers

A **mixed number** is made up of a whole number and a fraction. These fraction bars represent a mixed number.

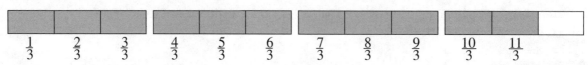

$\frac{1}{3}$ $\frac{2}{3}$ $\frac{3}{3}$ $\frac{4}{3}$ $\frac{5}{3}$ $\frac{6}{3}$ $\frac{7}{3}$ $\frac{8}{3}$ $\frac{9}{3}$ $\frac{10}{3}$ $\frac{11}{3}$

There are 3 whole figures shaded. The last figure is $\frac{2}{3}$ shaded. So, $3\frac{2}{3}$ figures are shaded. Or, you can say $\frac{11}{3}$ of the figures are shaded.

Directions

Write a mixed number for each picture.

1.
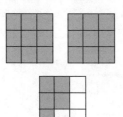

_____

2.

_____

3.
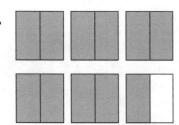

_____

4.
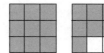

_____

Directions

Write each fraction as a mixed number.
Use fraction bars to help you.

5. $\frac{11}{2} =$ _____

6. $\frac{15}{7} =$ _____

7. $\frac{13}{4} =$ _____

8. $\frac{10}{3} =$ _____

Assessment

Directions

Write each fraction in simplest form.

1. $\frac{3}{6}$ = _____

2. $\frac{8}{12}$ = _____

3. $\frac{6}{8}$ = _____

Directions

Write each fraction as a mixed number.

4. $\frac{8}{3}$ = _____

5. $\frac{11}{9}$ = _____

6. $\frac{13}{4}$ = _____

Directions

Find the common denominator.

7. $\frac{1}{2}$ and $\frac{2}{3}$

8. $\frac{1}{4}$ and $\frac{3}{8}$

_____   _____

Directions

Add or subtract. Reduce to simplest form.

9. $\begin{array}{r} \frac{1}{5} \\ + \frac{3}{5} \\ \hline \end{array}$

10. $\begin{array}{r} \frac{3}{6} \\ - \frac{1}{6} \\ \hline \end{array}$

11. $\begin{array}{r} 2\frac{1}{8} \\ + \frac{3}{8} \\ \hline \end{array}$

12. $\begin{array}{r} 6\frac{7}{9} \\ - 4 \\ \hline \end{array}$

13. $\begin{array}{r} 5\frac{1}{2} \\ + 2\frac{1}{10} \\ \hline \end{array}$

14. $\begin{array}{r} 3\frac{3}{4} \\ - 2\frac{5}{12} \\ \hline \end{array}$

15. $1\frac{4}{5} - \frac{2}{10}$ = _____

16. $6\frac{1}{2} + 2\frac{2}{4}$ = _____

Simplest Form

You can divide both the numerator and the denominator of a fraction by the same number to **simplify** the fraction.

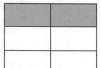 

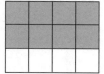 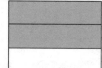

$\frac{2}{6} = \frac{2 \div 2}{6 \div 2} = \frac{1}{3}$.

$\frac{8}{12} = \frac{8 \div 4}{12 \div 4} = \frac{2}{3}$.

$\frac{2}{6}$ in simplest form is $\frac{1}{3}$.

$\frac{8}{12}$ in simplest form is $\frac{2}{3}$.

Complete to write $\frac{9}{36}$ in simplest form.

Step 1: Find a number that will divide evenly into both the numerator and the denominator.

$\frac{9}{36} = \frac{9 \div 3}{36 \div 3} = \frac{\square}{\square}$

Step 2: Repeat Step 1 until the only number that will divide both the numerator and the denominator is 1.

$\frac{3}{12} = \frac{3 \div 3}{12 \div 3} = \frac{\square}{\square}$

So, $\frac{9}{36}$ in simplest form is $\frac{1}{4}$.

Directions

Complete.

1.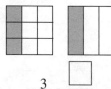

$\frac{3}{9} = \frac{\square}{3}$

2.

$\frac{4}{16} = \frac{\square}{4}$

3.

$\frac{8}{10} = \frac{\square}{5}$

4. $\frac{2}{4} = \frac{2 \div 2}{4 \div 2} = \frac{\square}{2}$

5. 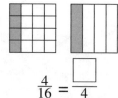 $\frac{6}{12} = \frac{6 \div 6}{12 \div 6} = \frac{\square}{2}$

6. 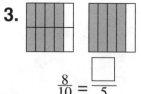 $\frac{6}{8} = \frac{6 \div 2}{8 \div 2} = \frac{\square}{4}$

Directions

Write each in simplest form.

7. $\frac{2}{14} =$ _____

8. $\frac{3}{18} =$ _____

9. $\frac{8}{28} =$ _____

Improper Fractions

An **improper fraction** has a numerator that is larger than the denominator. You can change an improper fraction to a mixed number by dividing.

$\frac{15}{4}$ are shaded.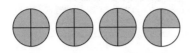

Step 1:
Divide the numerator by the denominator.

$$4\overline{)15}^{3} \\ \underline{-12} \\ 3$$

So, $\frac{15}{4} = 3\frac{3}{4}$.

Step 2:
Show how many fourths are left over.

$$3\frac{3}{4} \leftarrow \text{remainder} \\ \leftarrow \text{divisor} \\ 4\overline{)15} \\ \underline{-12} \\ 3$$

Directions

Write each improper fraction as a mixed number.

1. $\frac{14}{6} \longrightarrow 6\overline{)14} \longrightarrow$ _____

2. $\frac{29}{8} \longrightarrow 8\overline{)29} \longrightarrow$ _____

3. $\frac{17}{4} \longrightarrow 4\overline{)17} \longrightarrow$ _____

4. $\frac{20}{3} \longrightarrow 3\overline{)20} \longrightarrow$ _____

5. $\frac{11}{2} =$ _____

6. $\frac{15}{7} =$ _____

7. $\frac{14}{9} =$ _____

8. $\frac{13}{4} =$ _____

Estimating Sums and Differences

You can estimate the sums and differences of fractions. Fraction bars can help you.

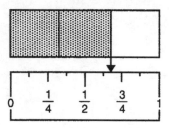

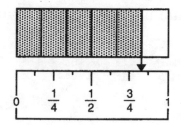

$\frac{2}{3}$ is about $\frac{1}{2}$.

$\frac{2}{3} + \frac{5}{6} = \square$

Think: $\frac{2}{3}$ is close to $\frac{1}{2}$.

$\frac{5}{6}$ is close to 1.

$\frac{1}{2} + 1 = 1\frac{1}{2}$

So, $\frac{2}{3} + \frac{5}{6}$ is about $1\frac{1}{2}$.

$\frac{5}{6}$ is about 1.

$\frac{5}{6} - \frac{2}{3} = \square$

Think: $\frac{5}{6}$ is close to 1.

$\frac{2}{3}$ is close to $\frac{1}{2}$.

So, $\frac{5}{6} - \frac{2}{3}$ is about $\frac{1}{2}$.

Directions

Use the fraction bar to help you estimate. Write *about 0, about $\frac{1}{2}$,* or *about 1.*

1.

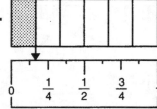

$\frac{1}{6}$ is _____.

2.

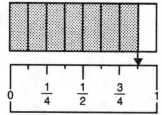

$\frac{7}{8}$ is _____.

3.

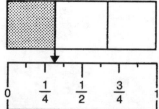

$\frac{1}{3}$ is _____.

Directions

Use the fraction bars on this worksheet to help you estimate each sum or difference. Write *about 0, about $\frac{1}{2}$, about 1,* or *about $1\frac{1}{2}$.*

4. $\frac{1}{6} + \frac{7}{8}$ **5.** $\frac{7}{8} - \frac{1}{3}$ **6.** $\frac{5}{6} - \frac{1}{6}$ **7.** $\frac{7}{8} + \frac{2}{3}$

_____   _____   _____   _____

Name _____ Date _____

Adding Fractions with Like Denominators

When you add like fractions, add only the numerators.

$\frac{2}{6} + \frac{2}{6} = \square$

 + =

$\dfrac{\text{2 parts shaded}}{\text{6 total parts}}$ + $\dfrac{\text{2 parts shaded}}{\text{6 total parts}}$ = $\dfrac{\text{4 parts shaded}}{\text{6 total parts}}$

Step 1: Add the numerators. $2 + 2 = 4$

Step 2: Write the denominator. $\frac{4}{6}$

Step 3: Reduce to simplest form if you can. $\frac{4}{6} = \frac{4 \div 2}{6 \div 2} = \frac{2}{3}$

So, $\frac{2}{6} + \frac{2}{6} = \frac{2}{3}$.

Directions

Color the correct number of parts. Then, solve.

1.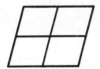

$\frac{1}{4} + \frac{2}{4} =$ _____

2.

$\frac{3}{8} + \frac{4}{8} =$ _____

3.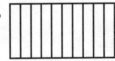

$\frac{2}{10} + \frac{5}{10} =$ _____

Directions

Add. Show how you add the numerators. Reduce to simplest form.

4. $\frac{2}{6} + \frac{2}{6} = \frac{2+2}{6} =$ _____

5. $\frac{3}{7} + \frac{3}{7} =$ _____

6. $\frac{1}{8} + \frac{3}{8} =$ _____

7. $\frac{2}{5} + \frac{2}{5} =$ _____

8. $\frac{2}{4} + \frac{1}{4} =$ _____

9. $\frac{1}{3} + \frac{1}{3} =$ _____

Adding Mixed Numbers with Like Denominators

When adding mixed numbers, first add the fractions and then add the whole numbers.

Find the sum.

Step 1	**Step 2**	**Step 3**
Add the fractions.	Add the whole numbers.	Reduce to simplest form.

$$7\frac{2}{6}$$
$$+\ 4\frac{2}{6}$$

$$7\frac{2}{6}$$
$$+\ 4\frac{2}{6}$$
$$\overline{\quad\frac{4}{6}}$$

$$7\frac{2}{6}$$
$$+\ 4\frac{2}{6}$$
$$\overline{11\frac{4}{6}}$$

$$7\frac{2}{6}$$
$$+\ 4\frac{2}{6}$$
$$\overline{11\frac{4}{6}} = 11\frac{2}{3}$$

So, the sum is $11\frac{2}{3}$.

If the problem is written horizontally, you can rewrite the problem vertically and then follow the steps above.

Write $3\frac{1}{7} + 4\frac{5}{7} = \boxed{} \longrightarrow$

$$3\frac{1}{7}$$
$$+\ 4\frac{5}{7}$$

$$3\frac{1}{7}$$
$$+\ 4\frac{5}{7}$$
$$\overline{7\frac{6}{7}}$$

Directions

Add. Reduce to simplest form.

1. $\quad 5\frac{2}{9}$
$\quad + 2\frac{4}{9}$

2. $\quad 3\frac{1}{6}$
$\quad + 7\frac{3}{6}$

3. $\quad 5\frac{3}{10}$
$\quad + \frac{6}{10}$

4. $\quad 7$
$\quad + 1\frac{3}{8}$

5. $5\frac{2}{8} + 6\frac{3}{8} = $ _____

6. $4 + \frac{2}{3} = $ _____

7. $3\frac{4}{7} + 2\frac{3}{7} = $ _____

8. $6\frac{1}{4} + \frac{2}{4} = $ _____

Subtracting Fractions with Like Denominators

When you subtract fractions with like denominators, subtract only the numerators.

$\frac{6}{8} - \frac{2}{8} = \square$

   −   =

$\dfrac{6 \text{ parts shaded}}{8 \text{ total parts}}$ − $\dfrac{2 \text{ parts shaded}}{8 \text{ total parts}}$ = $\dfrac{4 \text{ parts shaded}}{8 \text{ total parts}}$

Step 1: Subtract the numerators. $6 - 2 = 4$

Step 2: Write the denominator. $\frac{4}{8}$

Step 3: Reduce to simplest form if you can. $\frac{4}{8} = \frac{4 \div 4}{8 \div 4} = \frac{1}{2}$

So, $\frac{6}{8} - \frac{2}{8} = \frac{1}{2}$.

Directions

Cross out the correct number of parts. Then, solve. Reduce to simplest form.

1.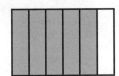

$\frac{5}{6} - \frac{3}{6} =$ _____

2.

$\frac{3}{6} - \frac{2}{6} =$ _____

Directions

Subtract. Show how you subtract the numerators. Reduce to simplest form.

3. $\frac{5}{6} - \frac{4}{6} = \frac{5-4}{6} =$ _____

4. $\frac{6}{7} - \frac{3}{7} =$ _____

5. $\frac{7}{8} - \frac{4}{8} =$ _____

6. $\frac{4}{5} - \frac{2}{5} =$ _____

7. $\frac{2}{4} - \frac{1}{4} =$ _____

8. $\frac{2}{3} - \frac{1}{3} =$ _____

Subtracting Mixed Numbers with Like Denominators

When subtracting mixed numbers, first subtract the fractions and then subtract the whole numbers.

Find the difference.	**Step 1:** Subtract the fractions.	**Step 2:** Subtract the whole numbers.	**Step 3:** Reduce to simplest form.
$8\frac{5}{6}$ $-\ 1\frac{3}{6}$	$8\frac{5}{6}$ $-\ 1\frac{3}{6}$ $\frac{2}{6}$	$8\frac{5}{6}$ $-\ 1\frac{3}{6}$ $7\frac{2}{6}$	$8\frac{5}{6}$ $-\ 1\frac{3}{6}$ $7\frac{2}{6} = 7\frac{1}{3}$

So, the difference is $7\frac{1}{3}$.

If the problem is written horizontally, you can rewrite the problem vertically and then follow the steps above.

Directions

Subtract. Reduce to simplest form.

1. $5\frac{4}{5}$ $-\ 1\frac{2}{5}$

2. $8\frac{6}{8}$ $-\ 3\frac{2}{8}$

3. $9\frac{8}{12}$ $-\ \frac{4}{12}$

4. $4\frac{5}{6}$ $-\ 3\frac{3}{6}$

5. $7\frac{8}{9}$ $-\ 6$

6. $9\frac{9}{10}$ $-\ 5\frac{2}{10}$

7. $8\frac{2}{4}$ $-\ 6\frac{1}{4}$

8. $3\frac{10}{12}$ $-\ 1\frac{7}{12}$

9. $7\frac{4}{5} - 1\frac{3}{5} =$ _____

10. $9\frac{5}{8} - 4 =$ _____

11. $5\frac{9}{12} - 2\frac{3}{12} =$ _____

12. $9\frac{2}{5} - \frac{1}{5} =$ _____

Name _____ Date _____

Common Denominators

Sometimes, it is necessary to find a **common denominator** when working with fractions. Fractions that have common denominators have the same denominator.

Find the common denominator of $\frac{1}{2}$ and $\frac{1}{6}$.

Step 1: Write equivalent fractions so that the fractions have a common denominator. Work with the fraction that has the smallest denominator first. Try to find a fraction that has the same denominator of the second fraction.

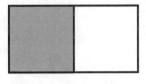 = 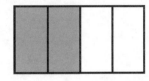 =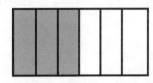

$\frac{1}{2}$ = $\frac{2}{4}$ = $\frac{3}{6}$

Step 2: Write the fractions with the same denominator. $\frac{3}{6}$ and $\frac{1}{6}$

So, sixths is the common denominator of $\frac{1}{2}$ and $\frac{1}{6}$.

Directions

Name the common denominator. Use fraction bars to help you. Then, write the fractions with the common denominator.

1. $\frac{2}{5}$ and $\frac{7}{10}$

_____

2. $\frac{2}{3}$ and $\frac{5}{6}$

_____

3. $\frac{1}{6}$ and $\frac{5}{12}$

_____

4. $\frac{1}{3}$ and $\frac{4}{9}$

_____

5. $\frac{3}{8}$ and $\frac{1}{4}$

_____

6. $\frac{2}{3}$ and $\frac{4}{6}$

_____

Adding Fractions with Unlike Denominators

When adding fractions, remember to look at the denominators first. If they are not the same, find a common denominator.

$\frac{3}{4} + \frac{1}{2} = \square$

Step 1:
Write equivalent fractions so that the fractions have a common denominator.

$$\frac{3}{4} \longrightarrow \frac{3}{4}$$
$$+\frac{1}{2} \longrightarrow \frac{2}{4}$$

Step 2:
Add the numerators. Write the sum with the same denominator.

$$\frac{3}{4}$$
$$+\frac{2}{4}$$
$$\overline{\frac{5}{4}}$$

Step 3:
Reduce to simplest form.

$$\frac{3}{4}$$
$$+\frac{2}{4}$$
$$\overline{\frac{5}{4}} = 1\frac{1}{4}$$

So, $\frac{3}{4} + \frac{1}{2} = 1\frac{1}{4}$.

Directions

Add. Use fraction bars. Reduce to simplest form.

1. $\frac{7}{10} \longrightarrow \boxed{}$
    $+\frac{1}{2} \longrightarrow \boxed{}$

2. $\frac{1}{9} \longrightarrow \boxed{}$
    $+\frac{1}{3} \longrightarrow \boxed{}$

3. $\frac{5}{8} \longrightarrow \boxed{}$
    $+\frac{1}{4} \longrightarrow \boxed{}$

4. $\frac{3}{4} \longrightarrow \boxed{}$
    $+\frac{3}{8} \longrightarrow \boxed{}$

5. $\frac{1}{4}$
    $+\frac{6}{16}$

6. $\frac{3}{5}$
    $+\frac{6}{10}$

26

Adding Mixed Numbers with Unlike Denominators

When adding mixed numbers, remember to look at the denominators first. If they are not the same, find a common denominator. Then, add the fractions. Next, add the whole numbers. Last, reduce to simplest form.

Example: $3\frac{1}{6} \longrightarrow 3\frac{1}{6}$

$\underline{+2\frac{1}{2} \longrightarrow 2\frac{3}{6}}$

$\qquad 5\frac{4}{6} = 5\frac{2}{3}$

Directions

Add. Reduce to simplest form.

1. $3\frac{2}{5} \longrightarrow$

$\underline{+2\frac{1}{10} \longrightarrow}$ _____

2. $6\frac{1}{3} \longrightarrow$

$\underline{+2\frac{1}{12} \longrightarrow}$ _____

3. $2\frac{3}{8}$

$\underline{+3\frac{1}{4}}$

4. $4\frac{1}{3}$

$\underline{+3\frac{1}{6}}$

5. $1\frac{5}{12}$

$\underline{+2\frac{1}{6}}$

6. $3\frac{5}{8}$

$\underline{+3\frac{1}{4}}$

7. $7\frac{2}{3} + 1\frac{2}{6} =$ _____

8. $8\frac{2}{9} + 1\frac{1}{3} =$ _____

Subtracting Fractions with Unlike Denominators

When subtracting fractions, remember to look at the denominators first. If they are not the same, find a common denominator.

$$\frac{5}{6} - \frac{1}{2} = \boxed{}$$

Step 1:
Write equivalent fractions so that the fractions have a common denominator.

$$\frac{5}{6} \rightarrow \frac{5}{6}$$
$$-\frac{1}{2} \rightarrow \frac{3}{6}$$

Step 2:
Subtract the numerators. Write the difference with the same denominator.

$$\frac{5}{6}$$
$$-\frac{3}{6}$$
$$\overline{\quad\frac{2}{6}\quad}$$

Step 3:
Reduce to simplest form.

$$\frac{5}{6}$$
$$-\frac{3}{6}$$
$$\overline{\quad\frac{2}{6} = \frac{1}{3}\quad}$$

So, $\frac{5}{6} - \frac{1}{2} = \frac{1}{3}$.

Directions

Subtract. Use fraction bars. Reduce to simplest form.

1. $\frac{9}{16} \rightarrow \boxed{}$

    $-\frac{1}{4} \rightarrow \boxed{}$

2. $\frac{3}{4} \rightarrow \boxed{}$

    $-\frac{5}{8} \rightarrow \boxed{}$

3. $\frac{2}{4} \rightarrow \boxed{}$

    $-\frac{1}{8} \rightarrow \boxed{}$

4. $\frac{9}{12} \rightarrow \boxed{}$

    $-\frac{3}{4} \rightarrow \boxed{}$

5. $\frac{12}{15}$

    $-\frac{2}{5}$

6. $\frac{1}{2}$

    $-\frac{2}{12}$

Subtracting Mixed Numbers with Unlike Denominators

When subtracting mixed numbers, remember to look at the denominators first. If they are not the same, find a common denominator. Then, subtract the fractions. Next, subtract the whole numbers. Last, reduce to simplest form.

Example:

$$4\frac{5}{6} \longrightarrow 4\frac{5}{6}$$
$$-2\frac{1}{2} \longrightarrow 2\frac{3}{6}$$
$$2\frac{2}{6} = 2\frac{1}{3}$$

Directions

Subtract. Reduce to simplest form.

1. $3\frac{7}{10} \longrightarrow$
$-1\frac{2}{5} \longrightarrow$

2. $5\frac{3}{4} \longrightarrow$
$-2\frac{1}{8} \longrightarrow$

3. $9\frac{5}{6}$
$-4\frac{2}{3}$

4. $3\frac{5}{12}$
$-2\frac{1}{4}$

5. $5\frac{1}{2}$
$-3\frac{3}{8}$

6. $3\frac{1}{2}$
$-2\frac{1}{8}$

7. $5\frac{4}{5} - 3\frac{3}{10} =$ _____

8. $6\frac{7}{12} - 3\frac{1}{2} =$ _____

Fraction of a Number

You can find the fraction of a number.

Find $\frac{2}{3}$ of 9.

Step 1:
Multiply the numerator by the number of items.

$2 \times 9 = 18$

Step 2:
Divide the product by the denominator.

$18 \div 3 = 6$

So, $\frac{2}{3}$ of 9 = 6.

Directions

Color each part.

1. Find $\frac{1}{2}$ of 8.

2. Find $\frac{2}{5}$ of 10.

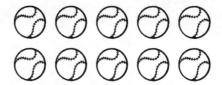

Directions

Solve.

3. $\frac{1}{3}$ of 27 = _____

4. $\frac{3}{5}$ of 15 = _____

5. $\frac{3}{4}$ of 16 = _____

6. $\frac{2}{7}$ of 14 = _____

Directions

Use a calculator to solve.

7. $\frac{2}{3}$ of 36 = _____

8. $\frac{3}{4}$ of 60 = _____

Assessment

Directions

Solve.

1. Alan uses $\frac{1}{4}$ cup of walnuts to make nutbread and $\frac{3}{8}$ cup to make the pineapple delight. How many cups of walnuts does he use in all?

_____

2. Jason swam in 8 out of 9 meets. Becky swam in 4 out of 9 meets. Who swam in about one half of the meets?

_____

3. 9 cups = _____ pints

4. 5 quarts = _____ gallons

Directions

Write or draw what comes next.

5. $\frac{1}{4}, \frac{2}{6}, \frac{3}{8}$, _____

6.  _____

Directions

Use the graph to answer the questions.

Mr. Alholm works in a men's shoe store. The graph shows the number of shoes he sold on Tuesday.

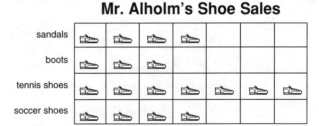

Mr. Alholm's Shoe Sales

= 2 shoes (1pair)

7. How many pairs of shoes did Mr. Alholm sell in all? _____

8. What fraction of soccer shoes did he sell? _____

9. What fraction of boots did he sell? _____

Word Problems

Directions

Solve.

1. It takes Brian 40 minutes to bake a casserole. In simplest form, what part of an hour is 40 minutes?

    _____

2. Mrs. Ho cut an apple pie into 8 equal pieces. Ben ate 3 pieces. What fraction of the apple pie was not eaten?

    _____

3. Samuru has a collection of 15 model cars. Three fifths are sports cars. How many of his cars are sports cars?

    _____

4. Alex eats $\frac{2}{8}$ of a muffin. Jed eats $\frac{1}{4}$ of the same muffin. Who eats more?

    _____

5. Alan is making a pineapple delight for dessert. He needs $\frac{3}{4}$ cup of pineapple. He has $\frac{1}{2}$ cup of pineapple. How many cups of pineapple does he still need?

    _____

6. A scout troop hiked along a trail. The scouts hiked $\frac{2}{8}$ of the way on the first day and $\frac{3}{8}$ of the way on the second day. What part of the trail did they hike in the two days?

    _____

7. A $2\frac{2}{3}$-mile bicycle race is held on a $\frac{1}{3}$-mile track. How many times must the racers go around the track to complete the race?

    _____

8. Jayce had a board that was $8\frac{3}{4}$ feet long. He cut off $2\frac{1}{2}$ feet to make a shelf. How much was left of the board?

    _____

Patterns

Directions

Answer the questions.

1.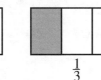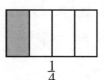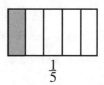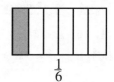

$\frac{1}{2}$ $\qquad$ $\frac{1}{3}$ $\qquad$ $\frac{1}{4}$ $\qquad$ $\frac{1}{5}$ $\qquad$ $\frac{1}{6}$

a. What is the pattern?

_____

b. What do you notice about the shaded parts?

_____

2.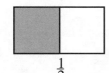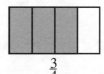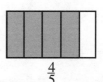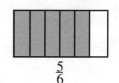

$\frac{1}{2}$ $\qquad$ $\frac{2}{3}$ $\qquad$ $\frac{3}{4}$ $\qquad$ $\frac{4}{5}$ $\qquad$ $\frac{5}{6}$

a. What is the pattern?

_____

b. What do you notice about the shaded parts?

_____

Directions

Complete the pattern.

3.

4.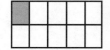

5. $\frac{1}{4}, \frac{2}{8}, \frac{3}{12},$ _____

6. $\frac{1}{2}, 1, 1\frac{1}{2}, 2,$ _____

7. $\frac{5}{6}, \frac{4}{6}, \frac{3}{6},$ _____

8. $\frac{1}{2}, \frac{2}{5}, \frac{3}{8}, \frac{4}{11},$ _____

Time

Directions

On each clock face, draw hands so that you can shade in a region that matches the given fraction. Under each clock face, write the time. For example, 5:00 could represent $\frac{5}{12}$ or $\frac{7}{12}$ depending on which region you shade.

1. $\frac{1}{2}$

_____

2. $\frac{1}{3}$

_____

3. $\frac{1}{4}$

_____

Directions

Use the time schedule to answer the questions.

Exhibits at Jamestown Colonial Village

Spinning Exhibit	Candle-Making Exhibit	Furniture-Making Exhibit	Tool-Making Exhibit
A.M. 10:00–10:45 11:30–12:15	A.M. 9:30–11:00	A.M. 10:00–11:00	A.M. 9:45–10:30 10:45–11:30
P.M. 2:15–3:00 3:30–4:15	P.M. 1:00–2:30	P.M. 1:00–2:00 3:00–4:00	P.M. 3:00–3:45

4. Kara went to watch the 10:00 A.M. spinning exhibit and the 10:45 tool-making exhibit. What fraction of time did Kara spend at the exhibits?

_____

5. John gets to the village at 1:00 P.M. He plans to stay for $2\frac{3}{4}$ hours. What exhibits might he see?

_____

6. How long does the candle-making exhibit last? Write the time as a fraction.

_____

Name _____   Date _____

Measurement

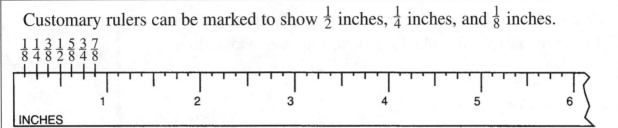

Customary rulers can be marked to show $\frac{1}{2}$ inches, $\frac{1}{4}$ inches, and $\frac{1}{8}$ inches.

$\frac{1}{8}$ $\frac{1}{4}$ $\frac{3}{8}$ $\frac{1}{2}$ $\frac{5}{8}$ $\frac{3}{4}$ $\frac{7}{8}$

INCHES

So, the straw is $3\frac{1}{2}$ in. long to the nearest $\frac{1}{2}$ inch.

Directions

Use a customary ruler to measure each to the nearest unit. Use $\frac{1}{2}$ inch, $\frac{1}{4}$ inch, or $\frac{1}{8}$ inch.

1. _____

2. _____

Directions

Name an object that measures about

3. 3 inches long. _____

4. $\frac{3}{4}$ inch wide. _____

Directions

Estimate the length of each object. Then, measure each. Find the difference between the estimate and the measurement. Complete the table.

	Object	Estimate	Measure	Difference
5.	Your middle finger			
6.	Your math book			
7.	Your shoe			

Name _____ Date _____

Capacity

Fractions are often used to name amounts of capacity measures. To weigh capacity or volume, use cups, quarts, and gallons.

1 pint = 2 cups
1 quart = 2 pints or 4 cups
1 gallon = 4 quarts, 8 pints, or 16 cups

Example: 3 cups = ☐ pints

| 1 pint | $\frac{1}{2}$ pint |

So, 3 cups = $1\frac{1}{2}$ pints.

Directions

Write the fraction.

1. 5 cups = _____ pints

2. 3 pints = _____ quarts

3. 12 pints = _____ gallons

4. 7 cups = _____ quarts

5. 8 cups = _____ quarts

6. 9 quarts = _____ gallons

Directions

Complete the table.

7. Yumiko has only a $\frac{1}{4}$-cup measuring spoon. Complete the table to tell how many times Yumiko must fill the measuring spoon to get the correct amount of flour.

Amount of flour needed	$\frac{1}{2}$ cup	1 cup	$1\frac{1}{4}$ cups	2 cups
Number of spoonfuls				

Make a Model

You can make a model to help solve the problem. Use fraction bars to model the fractions. Line up the fraction bars so you can tell which bar is the largest and which bar is the smallest.

Example: Beth made a snack mix for the class party. She used $\frac{1}{2}$ lb of peanuts, $\frac{2}{3}$ lb of pretzels, and $\frac{1}{4}$ lb of dried fruit. List the ingredients in order from greatest to least amount.

$\frac{1}{2}$ lb of peanuts

$\frac{2}{3}$ lb of pretzels

$\frac{1}{4}$ lb of dried fruit

The bar for pretzels is the largest and the bar for dried fruit is the smallest. So, the ingredients in order from greatest to least are pretzels, peanuts, and dried fruit.

Directions

Make a model to solve.

1. The amusement park has a colorful sidewalk. After the first square, every third square is orange, and every fifth square is green. Draw a model of the first 12 squares below. What fraction of the first 12 squares is either orange or green?

2. Patti made punch from $\frac{1}{2}$ gallon of grape juice, $\frac{2}{3}$ gallon of kiwi juice, and $\frac{5}{8}$ gallon of papaya juice. Draw a model for each in the space below. Then list the ingredients in order from greatest to least.

_____

_____

_____

_____

Bar Graphs

A **bar graph** uses bars to show information. The bars can be vertical or horizontal. The heights and lengths of the bars make it easier to compare data.

The bar graph shows the pets that students in Miss Moreno's fourth-grade class have at home.

To read a bar graph, follow these steps.

Step 1: Find a category name. Move your finger to the end of the bar for that group.

Step 2: Move your finger from the end of the bar to the scale of numbers. Read the number.

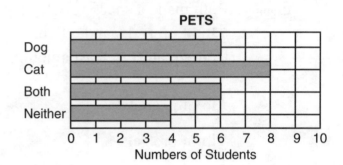

(Directions)

Use the graph to answer the questions.

1. What pet did most students have? _____

2. What pet did the same number of students have? _____

3. How many students are in Miss Moreno's class? _____

4. Write in simplest form the fraction of students who have

   a. dogs. _____   **b.** cats. _____

   c. both animals. _____   **d.** neither animal. _____

Name _____ Date _____

Circle Graphs

A **circle graph** looks like it sounds. Each slice of the circle is a piece of information included in the circle. The size of each piece shows its relationship to the whole and to each piece in the circle. A circle graph can use fractions to show data. The sum of the fractional pieces must equal 1.

The graph shows the fractional amount of trash Kim picks up at the beach.

Items Kim Picks Up

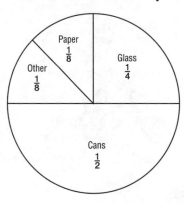

Directions

Use the graph to answer the questions.

1. What fraction of glass did Kim pick up? _____

2. What fraction of paper and glass did Kim pick up? _____

3. Did Kim pick up more cans or glass? How much more?

_____

4. If Kim picks up 24 pounds of trash, write the amount of each category as a weight.

a. glass _____ **b.** cans _____

c. other _____ **d.** paper _____

Name _____ Date _____

Line Graphs

A **line graph** shows how data changes over time. The scale runs along the left side of the graph. The time period is set along the bottom of the graph. If the points of the line graph are between numbers of the scale, you will need to estimate.

The line graph shows the bicycles sold in one week at a sports store.

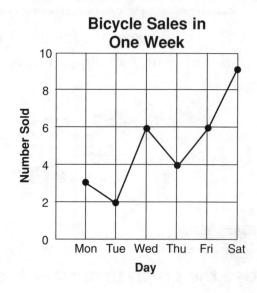

Bicycle Sales in One Week

Directions

Use the graph to answer the questions.

1. On what day were the least number of bicycles sold? _____

2. On what days were the same number of bicycles sold? _____

3. How many bicycles were sold in all? _____

4. Write in simplest form the fraction of bicycles sold

   a. on Wednesday. _____   **b.** on Tuesday. _____

   c. on Monday. _____   **d.** on Saturday. _____

Probability

The spinner can stop on a star, a square, or a triangle. You can write a fraction for the probability of the spinner landing on a star.

$\dfrac{3}{8}$ ← number of stars
← total number of shapes

So, the probability of landing on a star is 3 out of 8, or $\frac{3}{8}$.

Directions

Look at the spinner. Find the probability of landing on each shape.

1. star

☐ ← number of stars
☐ ← total number of shapes

2. square

☐ ← number of squares
☐ ← total number of shapes

3. triangle

_____

4. circle

_____

Directions

Look at the bag. Find the probability of picking a marble of each color.

5. black _____

6. striped _____

7. white _____

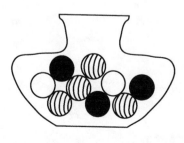

Algebra

A letter can take the place of a number in a number sentence. The letter represents the number for which you solve.

Example: $\frac{1}{2} + x = \frac{3}{4}$

$x = \frac{1}{4}$

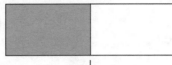

Check: $\frac{1}{2} + \frac{1}{4} = \frac{3}{4}$

$\frac{1 \times 2}{2 \times 2} + \frac{1}{4} = \frac{3}{4}$

$\frac{2}{4} + \frac{1}{4} = \frac{3}{4}$

$\frac{3}{4} = \frac{3}{4}$

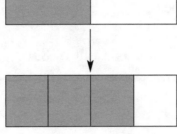

Directions

Use fraction bars to help you solve. Reduce to simplest form.

1. $\frac{1}{2} + \frac{2}{6} = n$

$n =$ _____

2. $\frac{9}{12} - \frac{1}{2} = x$

$x =$ _____

3. $\frac{5}{6} - \frac{2}{12} = r$

$r =$ _____

4. $\frac{1}{3} + \frac{5}{12} = s$

$s =$ _____

5. $\frac{5}{9} + \frac{1}{3} = y$

$y =$ _____

6. $\frac{3}{4} - \frac{3}{8} = p$

$p =$ _____

Fraction Codes

Directions

Decode the message. Each fraction in the message can be found on one of the number lines. Locate the point for each fraction. Write the letter of that point below the fraction in the message.

1.
                E
●———————————●———————————●
            halves

2.
            A   D   I
●———————●———————●———————●———————●
            fourths

3.
I   G   R   N
●———●———●———●———●———●———●
        sixths

4.
S   O   A
●———●———●———●———●———●———●———●
        eights

5.
        U   Y   T
●———————●———————●———————●
        thirds

6.
S   J   P
●———————●———————●———————●———————●
        fifths

7.
    A   T   R
●———●———●———●———●———●———●———●
        sevenths

8.
                F   T   B C
●—●—●—●—●—●—●—●—●—●
        tenths

The message:

 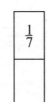 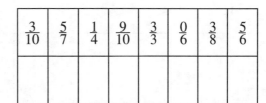

$\frac{3}{5}$	$\frac{1}{3}$	$\frac{3}{4}$	$\frac{2}{6}$	$\frac{1}{2}$

$\frac{1}{7}$

$\frac{3}{10}$	$\frac{5}{7}$	$\frac{1}{4}$	$\frac{9}{10}$	$\frac{3}{3}$	$\frac{0}{6}$	$\frac{3}{8}$	$\frac{5}{6}$

$\frac{8}{10}$	$\frac{2}{3}$

$\frac{4}{4}$	$\frac{3}{7}$	$\frac{0}{8}$

$\frac{4}{5}$	$\frac{6}{8}$	$\frac{3}{6}$	$\frac{6}{10}$	$\frac{0}{5}$

Name _____ Date _____

Fractions and Decimals

A **decimal** is a number that uses place value and a decimal point to show a value less than 1. A fraction can name a decimal.

Model	Fraction	Decimal			Read
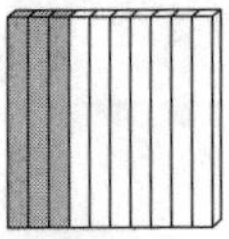	3 shaded parts / 10 parts	O 0	T 3	H	three tenths
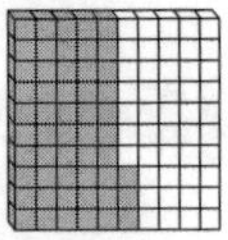	53 shaded parts / 100 parts	O 0	T 5	H 3	fifty-three hundredths

Directions

Complete the table.

	Model	Fraction	Decimal			Read
1.		☐ shaded parts ☐ parts	O	T	H	
2.			O	T	H	
3. 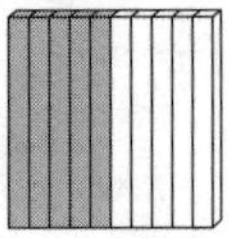			O	T	H	

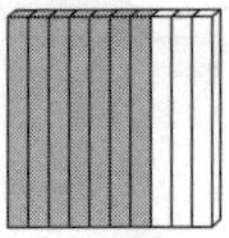

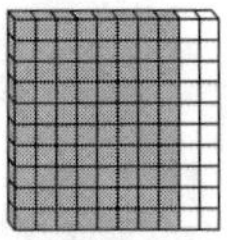

Name _____ Date _____

Money

The value of money can be written as a fraction or as a decimal.	100 pennies = 1 dollar 20 nickels = 1 dollar 10 dimes = 1 dollar 4 quarters = 1 dollar

Directions

Write a fraction and a decimal to tell what part of each coin makes a dollar. Write the fractions in simplest form.

1. a penny

_____

2. a nickel

_____

3. a dime

_____

4. a quarter

_____

Directions

Write each amount as a fraction and as a decimal.

5.

_____

6.

_____

The hobby shop is having a sale on stamp albums. $\frac{1}{3}$ of $15 = $5   You save $5.

Directions

Write the amount saved.

7. Regular Price: $9

$\frac{1}{3}$ off _____

8. Regular Price: $24

$\frac{1}{2}$ off _____

Geometry

Name _____ Date _____

Directions

Write the fraction of shaded parts in simplest form.

1.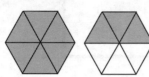

2.

_____   _____

Directions

Write a mixed number in simplest form for each of the following figures. The figure at the right stands for 1.

3.

4.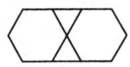

_____   _____

5.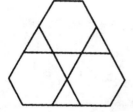

6.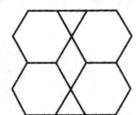

7.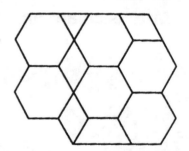

_____   _____   _____

Directions

Shade parts of the following figures. Have a partner write a mixed number that tells how much is shaded.

8.

9.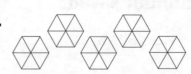

_____   _____

Fractions: Concepts and Problem Solving
Grade 4

Answer Key

p. 5
1. C
2. C
3. C
4. B
5. C
6. D
7. B
8. A

p. 6
9. D
10. B
11. B
12. A
13. C
14. B
15. C
16. D

p. 7
1. 2/5
2. 5/8
3. 1/8
4. 3/5
5. one half; one out of two; one divided by two
6. three fourths; three out of four; three divided by four
7. Students circle the figure showing 4/8.; 2/4 = 4/8
8. <
9. >

p. 8
1. part of a group
2. part of a whole
3. part of a group
4. Students circle the first and third figures.
5. one quarter; one out of four; one divided by four
6. two thirds; two out of three; two divided by three
7. four ninths; four out of nine; four divided by nine

p. 9
1. Students color the second and fourth shapes.
2. Students color the second and fourth shapes.
3. shaded: 3; total parts: 5
4. shaded: 1; total parts: 2
5. shaded: 1; total parts: 3
6. shaded: 3; total parts: 4

p. 10
1. parts with cats: 2; total parts: 3
2. parts with stars: 7; total parts: 9
3. 3/6
4. 4/9

p. 11
1. about 1/2
2. about 0
3. about 1
4. 1/4
5. 2/3
6. 1/3

p. 12
1. equal
2. not equal
3. not equal
4. not equal
5. equal
6. not equal

p. 13
1. 1
2. 1
3. 4
4. 1
5. Students shade 1 part.; 1/2
6. Students shade 3 parts.; 3/6

p. 14
1. >
2. <
3. =
4. <
5. >
6. <
7. >
8. <
9. =

p. 15
1. 3/8, 5/8, 6/8
2. 2/5, 2/3, 7/9
3. 1/5, 2/5, 3/5
4. 1/4, 2/6, 2/5
5. 1/6, 1/3, 1/2
6. 5/8, 2/3, 3/4
7. When the denominators are the same, the greater the numerator, the greater the fraction.
8. When the numerators are the same, the greater the denominator, the smaller the fraction.

p. 16
1. 2 5/9
2. 1 3/8
3. 5 1/2
4. 1 7/9
5. 5 1/2
6. 2 1/7
7. 3 1/4
8. 3 1/3

p. 17
1. 1/2
2. 2/3
3. 3/4
4. 2 2/3
5. 1 2/9
6. 3 1/4
7. 6
8. 8
9. 4/5
10. 1/3
11. 2 1/2
12. 2 7/9
13. 7 3/5
14. 1 1/3
15. 1 3/5
16. 9

p. 18
1. 1
2. 1
3. 4
4. 1
5. 1
6. 3
7. 1/7
8. 1/6
9. 2/7

p. 19
1. 2 2/6
2. 3 5/8
3. 4 1/4
4. 6 2/3
5. 5 1/2
6. 2 1/7
7. 1 5/9
8. 3 1/4

p. 20
1. about 0
2. about 1
3. about 1/2
4. about 1
5. about 1/2
6. about 1
7. about 1 1/2

p. 21
For 1–3, check students' coloring.
1. 3/4
2. 7/8
3. 7/10
For 4–9, check students' adding.
4. 2/3
5. 6/7
6. 1/2
7. 4/5
8. 3/4
9. 2/3

p. 22
1. 7 2/3
2. 10 2/3
3. 5 9/10
4. 8 3/8
5. 11 5/8
6. 4 2/3
7. 6
8. 6 3/4

p. 23
For 1–2, check students' coloring.
1. 1/3
2. 1/6
For 3–8, check students' subtracting.
3. 1/6
4. 3/7
5. 3/8
6. 2/5
7. 1/4
8. 1/3

p. 24
1. 4 2/5
2. 5 1/2
3. 9 1/3
4. 1 1/3
5. 1 8/9
6. 4 7/10
7. 2 1/4
8. 2 1/4
9. 6 1/5
10. 5 5/8
11. 3 1/2
12. 9 1/5

p. 25
1. tenths; 4/10 and 7/10
2. sixths; 4/6 and 5/6
3. twelfths; 2/12 and 5/12
4. ninths; 3/9 and 4/9
5. eighths; 3/8 and 2/8
6. sixths; 4/6 and 4/6

Fractions: Concepts and Problem Solving
Grade 4

Answer Key (cont.)

p. 26
1. 7/10 + 5/10 = 12/10 = 1 1/5
2. 1/9 + 3/9 = 4/9
3. 5/8 + 2/8 = 7/8
4. 6/8 + 3/8 = 9/8 = 1 1/8
5. 5/8
6. 1 1/5

p. 27
1. 3 4/10 + 2 1/10 = 5 1/2
2. 6 4/12 + 2 1/12 = 8 5/12
3. 5 5/8
4. 7 1/2
5. 3 7/12
6. 6 7/8
7. 9
8. 9 5/9

p. 28
1. 9/16 – 4/16 = 5/16
2. 6/8 – 5/8 = 1/8
3. 4/8 – 1/8 = 3/8
4. 9/12 – 9/12 = 0
5. 2/5
6. 1/3

p. 29
1. 3 7/10 – 1 4/10 = 2 3/10
2. 5 6/8 – 2 1/8 = 3 5/8
3. 5 1/6
4. 1 1/6
5. 2 1/8
6. 1 3/8
7. 2 1/2
8. 3 1/12

p. 30
1. Students color 4.
2. Students color 4.
3. 9
4. 9
5. 12
6. 4
7. 24
8. 45

p. 31
1. 5/8 cup
2. Becky
3. 4 1/2
4. 1 1/4
5. 4/10
6.
7. 18
8. 2/9
9. 1/6

p. 32
1. 2/3 of an hour
2. 5/8
3. 9 sports cars
4. They eat the same amount.
5. 1/4 cup
6. 5/8 of the trail
7. 8 times
8. 6 1/4 feet

p. 33
1. a. The denominator increases by 1.
   b. They get smaller as the denominator gets larger.
2. a. The numerator and the denominator increase by 1.
   b. The shaded area gets larger as both numbers get larger.
3. Students shade all 5 parts.
4. Students shade the first and third squares on the top row and the second and fourth squares on the bottom row.
5. 4/16
6. 2 1/2
7. 2/6
8. 5/14

p. 34
1. Answers will vary. Possible answer: 6:00.
2. Answers will vary. Possible answer: 4:00.
3. Answers will vary. Possible answer: 3:00.
4. 1 1/2 hours
5. Answers will vary. Possible answer: furniture-making, spinning, tool-making.
6. 1 1/2 hours

p. 35
1. 2 7/8 in.
2. 2 3/8 in.
3. Answers will vary.
4. Answers will vary.
For 5–7, check students' work.

p. 36
1. 2 1/2
2. 1 1/2
3. 1 1/2
4. 1 3/4
5. 2
6. 2 1/4
7. 2; 4; 5; 8

p. 37
1.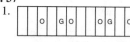
6/12 of the first 12 squares are either orange or green.
2. grape juice

kiwi juice

papaya juice

p. 38
1. cat
2. dog and both a cat and dog
3. 24
4. a. 1/4
   b. 1/3
   c. 1/4
   d. 1/6

p. 39
1. 1/4
2. 3/8
3. cans; 1/4
4. a. 6 lb.
   b. 12 lb.
   c. 3 lb.
   d. 3 lb.

p. 40
1. Tuesday
2. Wednesday and Friday
3. 30
4. a. 1/5
   b. 1/15
   c. 1/10
   d. 3/10

p. 41
1. 5/8
2. 1/4
3. 1/6
4. 2/5
5. 3/9 or 1/3
6. 4/9
7. 2/9

p. 42
1. 5/6
2. 1/4
3. 2/3
4. 3/4
5. 8/9
6. 3/8

p. 43
Message: Judge a fraction by its parts.

p. 44
1. 7/10; 0.7; seven tenths
2. 80/100; 0.80; eighty hundredths
3. 5/10; 0.5; five tenths

p. 45
1. 1/100; 0.01
2. 1/20; 0.05
3. 1/10; 0.10
4. 1/4; 0.25
5. 56/100; 0.56
6. 1 35/100; 1.35
7. $3.00
8. $12.00

p. 46
1. 1 1/2
2. 2 1/6
3. 1 1/6
4. 2 1/3
5. 3 2/3
6. 4 2/3
7. 7 2/3
8. Answers will vary.
9. Answers will vary.